THE HELLO KITTY® BAKING BOOK

Recipes for Cookies, Cupcakes, Pies, and More

BY MICHELE CHEN CHOCK

QUIRK

© 2014 by Quirk Productions, Inc.

SANRIO, HELLO KITTY, and associated logos are trademarks and/or registered trademarks of Sanrio Co., Ltd.

© 1976, 1988, 1993, 1996, 2014 SANRIO CO., LTD.

ISBN 978-1-59474-706-9

Library of Congress Cataloging in Publication Number: 2013944075

Printed in China

Typeset in Verlag, Trend, HT Gelateria and Helvetica

Designed by Amanda Richmond

Photography by Steve Legato, except for the following pages by Michele Chen Chock; 1, 17, 19, 22, 27, 33, 34, 36, 41, 43, 51, 61, 63, 64, 67, 72, 81, 82, 83, 84, 85, 86, 96

Food and prop styling by Michele Chen Chock

Production management by John J. McGurk

Quirk Books
215 Church St.
Philadelphia, PA 19106

quirkbooks.com

10 9 8 7 6 5 4 3 2 1

CONTENTS

BAKING WITH HELLO KITTY

I've been baking all my life, ever since my mother taught me how to make breads and desserts. Baking has been my creative outlet and a way to share with friends and family. My favorite part is seeing how happy my homemade baked goods make people. And through my blog—I Heart Baking!—I've been able to share the techniques and recipes I've learned with even more people interested in creative baking.

I loved Hello Kitty as a little girl also. Just thinking of the whimsical characters created by Sanrio brings back warm memories of my childhood. When my own daughter was born, I wanted to introduce her to this innocent and happy world. So I started baking Hello Kitty cookies and cupcakes and cakes . . . soon it became a challenge to turn any dessert into a Hello Kitty dessert. I had discovered a way to combine my baking obsession with my Hello Kitty obsession, and it was wonderful!

In this book I share all of my desserts inspired by Hello Kitty and her adorable friends. You will find simple recipes for beginners as well as more challenging ones with multiple components, and many in between. So let's start baking with the cute and charming Hello Kitty!

GETTING STARTED

Baking is all about precise measurements, quality ingredients, and a few simple tools. Here's how to ensure your success in the kitchen.

Key Ingredients

Here's what to look for when you're shopping for some of the most common ingredients used in this book.

BUTTER: Unsalted butter is best for baking. It's often used at room temperature, which means it should be soft to the touch but not melted.

CREAM CHEESE: This is a lovely secret ingredient in baking, especially in frostings. Avoid using whipped or nonfat varieties, which won't create the same light, creamy texture.

EGGS: For these recipes, use large eggs unless otherwise specified. Soak the eggs in a warm water bath if you need to bring them to room temperature quickly.

EXTRACTS: Vanilla and almond extracts are common ingredients. Once in a while you may want to bake with peppermint or strawberry extract. Used in moderation, these extracts give a hint of extra flavor without overwhelming the dessert.

FLOUR: Most of these recipes call for regular all-purpose flour, but sometimes they call for cake flour, especially for vanilla cake, which is hard to make light and fluffy. Cake flour helps because it's softer and contains less gluten than all-purpose flour.

GEL-BASED FOOD COLORING: I prefer these because it takes only a few drops to make rich, vibrant colors. Plus it doesn't thin your frosting, as liquid food coloring tends to do.

MILK: Most of these recipes call for whole milk; however, I have used soymilk in the cake recipes when baking for kids with allergies. For ice cream or pudding, stick with whole milk or else the texture will not be the same.

SPRINKLES: Many recipes in this book call for rainbow sprinkles—which kids love! Heart-shaped sprinkles work well for Hello Kitty's bow, and they come in many colors for easy customization.

SUGAR: For cake and cookie recipes in this book, white granulated sugar is most commonly used. For the frostings and icings I prefer confectioners' (or powdered); its lighter consistency won't weigh them down (plus it won't be grainy). If a recipe calls for brown sugar, measure it packed; either light or dark brown sugar can be used, depending on how much of the molasses taste you prefer.

Baking Equipment

I recommend keeping all of these tools on hand for your baking ventures.

BAKING SHEETS: These wide pans have shallow rims and in this book they are used mainly for baking cookies and macarons. Line with parchment paper or silicone baking mats to prevent sticking and make cleanup easier.

CANDY THERMOMETER: When making anything that involves hot sugar, such as meringue, macarons, caramel, and candy, it's best to use a candy thermometer so that you know the exact temperature and when to remove the mixture from heat. Burning sugar can happen in mere seconds!

CAKE PANS: The most commonly used in these recipes are 8-inch and 6-inch pans, but I do use a 9-inch pan once in a while. Coat with baking spray and line with parchment paper rounds before pouring in batter—the cake will come out easily without tearing.

CAKE STANDS: When it comes to decorative serving stands, you can never have too many! I find that 10-inch types are the most versatile—big enough for an 8- or 9-inch cake but also perfect for a 6-inch cake or cupcakes. I also have a few that turn, making for the easy application of frosting. Look for ones that glide easily and have a heavy sturdy base.

COOKIE CUTTERS: These are so much fun to collect, especially Hello Kitty ones! Most are fairly inexpensive, and they can be used for many purposes, even as templates for piping shapes on cakes.

MIXER: I find stand mixers efficient because they allow for hands-free mixing so that you can measure your next ingredient or get an item from the pantry or fridge. But handheld mixers are fine too for the recipes in this book.

BOWLS AND SPOONS: I tend to use mainly stainless steel or glass mixing bowls, with rubber or silicone spatulas for mixing, stirring, and scraping that last bit of batter from the bowl. I like spatulas made in one piece; look for ones that can withstand high heat so you can use them for stirring custards and puddings.

PARCHMENT PAPER: This type of cellulose-based paper is nonstick, making it perfect for lining baking sheets and cake pans to ensure easy release.

STAMPERS: These tools are sometimes sold with cookie cutters and are great for adding facial definitions and other details to cookie and pie doughs.

Decorating Equipment

Once you've baked something delicious, it's time to decorate.

CAKE BOARDS: These are good for transporting baked goods from your workspace to the refrigerator and then to a plate or stand (with the board still underneath). They come in all sizes, but I most often use 6-, 8-, and 10-inch rounds.

DECORATING TIP COUPLERS: Couplers are little two-part tools made of a base and a ring; they let you change decorating tips without having to switch piping bags.

DECORATING TIPS: These come in all shapes and sizes to create an amazing variety of decorations. I most commonly use star tips, which pipe stars, shell borders, and decorative swirls. I use rounds tips, too—large ones for piping macarons or faces, and small ones for piping details like eyes and noses. Basket-weave tips allow you to pipe decorative patterns onto cupcakes or the sides of a cake, and leaf tips make leaves and triangular shapes (like Hello Kitty's ears).

DECORATING SQUEEZE BOTTLES: These are great for piping thinned icing onto cookies. I find that thin icing quickly oozes out of a piping bag and makes a mess, whereas squeeze bottles can be set upright and don't leak.

DISPOSABLE PIPING BAGS: Piping bags are used with tips to pipe frosting or icing. I prefer the disposable kind mainly because reusable bags often stay greasy inside even after washing.

LOLLIPOP STICKS: These are often sold as "candy sticks" or "treat sticks." I recommend the paper kind because they are sturdier and solid.

CARD STOCK, PAPER PLATES, OR OTHER HEAVY PAPER: Most any heavy paper will work well for making templates and homemade patterns for Hello Kitty and other cute shapes.

COOKIES ♥

HELLO KITTY SUGAR COOKIES WITH ROYAL ICING ...13

More to Try: My Melody, Hello Kitty's Bow, Flower, and Heart-Shaped Cookies

HELLO KITTY JACK-O-LANTERN SPICE COOKIES ...13

More to Try: Badtz-Maru, Keroppi, and Chococat Spice Cookies

HELLO KITTY FRENCH MACARONS ...18

More to Try: Mimmy Macarons, Hello Kitty Jam-Filled Macarons, and Hello Kitty Chocolate-Filled Macarons

HELLO KITTY MERINGUE COOKIES ...23

HELLO KITTY ICE CREAM SANDWICHES ...24

More to Try: Chocolate Sandwich Cookies

HELLO KITTY BROWNIES ...29

More to Try: My Melody, Pretty Bow, Flower, and Heart-Shaped Brownies

HELLO KITTY SUGAR COOKIES
WITH ROYAL ICING

Rich, buttery, and decorated with a thin layer of sweet royal icing, these classic sugar cookies are great for birthdays, holidays, or anytime snacks. Just be sure to give yourself plenty of time to make them—it's best to let the icing dry overnight.

COOKIES

1 cup sugar
14 tbsp (1¾ sticks) unsalted butter
1 egg, room temperature
1 tsp vanilla extract
3 cups all-purpose flour
Pinch salt

ICING AND DECORATING

1 tbsp dried egg white powder
⅓ cup water
4 cups (1 pound) confectioners'
  sugar
1 tbsp freshly squeezed lemon juice,
  strained
Gel-based food coloring
  (black, yellow, and your choice
  for the bow)

TO MAKE COOKIES: Combine sugar and butter in the bowl of a stand mixer. Using the paddle attachment, beat until smooth and creamy. Add egg and vanilla, mixing at medium speed until combined. Sift in flour and salt, then mix until flour is incorporated and dough starts to come together in a large mass. Turn out the dough onto a floured surface and press with your hands to flatten it into a disk. Wrap in plastic wrap and chill in the refrigerator for at least 20 minutes.

Preheat oven to 350°F; line a baking sheet with parchment paper. Place dough onto a floured surface and use a rolling pin to roll it out to a ⅛-inch thickness. Use cookie cutters to cut out shapes, then use a spatula to transfer them to the baking sheet. (Tip: If the dough gets warm and too soft to work with, chill for 30 minutes.) Bake for 10 to 12 minutes, or until golden brown. Let cool.

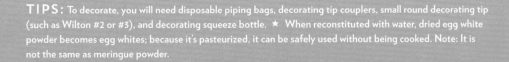

TIPS: To decorate, you will need disposable piping bags, decorating tip couplers, small round decorating tip (such as Wilton #2 or #3), and decorating squeeze bottle. ★ When reconstituted with water, dried egg white powder becomes egg whites; because it's pasteurized, it can be safely used without being cooked. Note: It is not the same as meringue powder.

TO MAKE ROYAL ICING: In a small bowl, dissolve dried egg white powder in water. Sift confectioners' sugar into the bowl of a stand mixer. Pour the dissolved egg whites and lemon juice through a strainer and into the confectioners' sugar. Mix with paddle attachment on high speed for about 5 minutes, or until becomes light and fluffy. Store icing in an airtight container at room temperature until ready to use.

TO ASSEMBLE: First, tint the icing different colors. In one bowl, place $1/3$ cup of the icing and stir in a few drops of yellow. In a second bowl, place $3/4$ cup of the icing and tint it black. Place $1 1/2$ cups of the icing in another bowl and tint it the color of your choice for the bow. Leave the rest of the icing white, for Hello Kitty's face. Next, make thinner icings to fill in the areas piped with thicker icing. To half of the white icing, add water a teaspoon at a time until thinned. Repeat for half of the bow icing. Fit piping bags with couplers and fill with one color of stiff icing. Fill each decorating squeeze bottle with the thinned icing.

Use the stiff bow icing to pipe the bow outline either freehand or using a paper template and edible food marker. Fill the bow shape by squeezing the thinned bow icing within the outline. Pipe stiff white icing around the cookie edge to outline Hello Kitty's face. Fill in face and ears with thinned white icing. (Use a toothpick to spread icing to edges of borders defined by the stiff icing.) Let dry overnight, uncovered, in a cool dry area. Leftover icing can be stored at room temperature in an airtight container; stir before using.

Once cookies are completely dry, use stiff black icing to pipe eyes and whiskers. Outline bow with either stiff bow-colored icing or stiff black icing. Use the yellow icing to pipe on the nose. Let dry.

Makes about 2 dozen cookies.

MORE TO TRY:
To make **My Melody**, **Hello Kitty's Bow, Flower,** or **Heart-Shaped Cookies,** use the corresponding cookie cutters to cut and bake shapes, then decorate accordingly.

HELLO KITTY JACK-O-LANTERN
SPICE COOKIES

These cinnamon ginger spice cookies are the perfect treat for fall. Each buttery cookie is topped with sweet royal icing and made to look like a Hello Kitty jack-o-lantern.

COOKIES

¹/₂ **cup sugar**
¹/₄ **cup packed brown sugar**
¹/₂ **cup (1 stick) unsalted butter**
1 egg, lightly beaten
2 cups all-purpose flour
1 tbsp ground cinnamon
1 tbsp ground ginger
¹/₈ **tsp ground cloves**

ICING AND DECORATING

1 recipe royal icing (page 13)
Gel-based food coloring
(orange, green, black)

TO MAKE COOKIES: Combine sugars and butter in the bowl of a standing mixer. Beat with a paddle attachment until creamy. Add egg and mix on medium speed until combined. Sift flour, cinnamon, ginger, and cloves into the mixture and mix until flour is incorporated and dough starts to come together in a large mass. Turn out dough onto a floured surface and flatten into a disk. Wrap in plastic wrap and chill in the refrigerator for at least 20 minutes.

Preheat the oven to 350°F; line a baking sheet with parchment paper. Place dough onto a floured surface and use a rolling pin to roll it to a little less than ¹/₈-inch thickness. Use a pumpkin cookie cutter to cut out shapes, then use a spatula to transfer them to the baking sheet. Bake for about 10 minutes, or until golden brown. Let cool.

TO DECORATE: In one bowl, place ¹/₂ cup of the icing and stir in a few drops of green coloring. In a

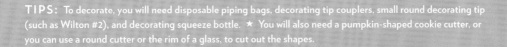

TIPS: To decorate, you will need disposable piping bags, decorating tip couplers, small round decorating tip (such as Wilton #2), and decorating squeeze bottle. ★ You will also need a pumpkin-shaped cookie cutter, or you can use a round cutter or the rim of a glass, to cut out the shapes.

second bowl, place ¼ cup of the icing and tint it black. Tint the remaining icing orange. To half of the orange icing, add water a teaspoon at a time until thinned. Fit each piping bag with a coupler and fill with one color of stiff icing. Fill the decorating squeeze bottle with the thinned orange icing.

Use the stiff orange icing to pipe the outline of the pumpkin (except the stem). Fill in the shape with the thinned orange icing. Use the stiff green icing to outline the stem, then pipe vertical lines or long zigzags to fill in the shape. Let dry overnight, uncovered, at room temperature.

When cookies are completely dry, use an edible food marker and a paper template to mark an outline of Hello Kitty's image in the middle of the pumpkin. Following the outline, use the stiff black icing to pipe the Hello Kitty image. Use stiff orange icing to outline the pumpkin once more, piping vertical curved lines on the pumpkin and stopping just above and below the Hello Kitty image. Let dry.

Makes about 18 cookies.

MORE TO TRY:
To make **Badtz-Maru, Keroppi,** or **Chococat Cookies**, use the corresponding template to outline and pipe the image.

HELLO KITTY
FRENCH MACARONS

Who could resist a French macaron in the shape of Hello Kitty?
These dainty almond cookies are as cute as they are delicious. The thin, crisp, and
perfectly tender centers give way to a tangy strawberry cream cheese filling.

MACARONS

²/₃ cup plus 2 tbsp sugar

2 tbsp plus 1 tsp water

4 egg whites, room temperature
and divided

1¹/₄ cups almond meal
(ground almonds)

1¹/₂ cups plus 1 tbsp confectioners'
sugar

FILLING AND
DECORATING

2 tbsp strawberry jam

1 recipe cream cheese frosting
(page 35)

About 1 tbsp red heart-shaped
sprinkles (about 80 sprinkles)

Black and yellow edible food markers

TO MAKE MACARON SHELLS: Add sugar
and water to a medium saucepan fitted with a candy
thermometer and bring to a boil, swirling mixture by
moving the saucepan, until the temperature reaches
245°F. (Tip: Don't stir. Stirring will crystallize the mixture
instead of keeping it smooth.) While the sugar mixture is
cooking, start whipping half the egg whites with an electric
mixer on medium speed until soft peaks form. When the
sugar mixture is ready, reduce mixer speed to low and
pour the hot sugar down the side of the mixing bowl into
the egg whites. Continue whisking at high speed until the
meringue becomes glossy and holds stiff peaks.

Combine almond meal and confectioners' sugar. Add
remaining egg whites, mixing with a rubber spatula until
combined. Fold in meringue in three additions. Continue

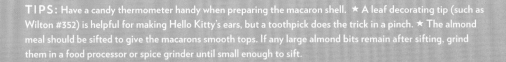

TIPS: Have a candy thermometer handy when preparing the macaron shell. ★ A leaf decorating tip (such as
Wilton #352) is helpful for making Hello Kitty's ears, but a toothpick does the trick in a pinch. ★ The almond
meal should be sifted to give the macarons smooth tops. If any large almond bits remain after sifting, grind
them in a food processor or spice grinder until small enough to sift.

TWO RED HEART-SHAPED SPRINKLES MAKE A CUTE BOW FOR HELLO KITTY! EDIBLE FOOD MARKERS (A.K.A. EDIBLE INK PENS) ARE ONE WAY TO EASILY DRAW ON THE COOKIE.

until mixture is well combined and has the consistency of a thick batter; it should not be too runny, but it should not be thick enough to hold peaks.

Line a baking sheet with parchment paper or a silicone baking mat. Fit a piping bag with a large round decorating tip and fill with batter. Reserve about $1/3$ cup of the batter if you plan to use the leaf tip for the ears. Pipe $1^1/2$-inch rounds of batter onto the baking sheet, spaced about $1/2$ inch apart.

Next, add ears onto half of the macaron shells (the bottom shells will not need ears). Fit a piping bag with a leaf tip, fill the bag with batter, and pipe on ears. Alternatively, use a toothpick and drag the batter out to form two pointy ears. Let shells rest for about 30 minutes at room temperature before baking. This will help form a nice shell.

Preheat oven to 325°F and bake for 14 to 15 minutes, until slightly golden. Let cool.

TO ASSEMBLE: Mix strawberry jam with frosting until well combined. Fit a piping bag with a large round decorating tip and fill with frosting. Place a bottom macaron shell (with no ears) upside down on a work surface and pipe a dollop of frosting in the center, leaving a narrow border. Place a top macaron shell (with ears) on top and gently press to evenly spread filling just to the edge of the shells.

TO DECORATE: Use a toothpick or a piping bag fitted with a small round tip to apply a bit of filling onto two red heart-shaped sprinkles and attach them just below the ear. Draw eyes and whiskers with black edible food marker and a nose with yellow edible food marker.

Refrigerate assembled macarons for at least 24 hours and up to 3 to 4 days. Bring to room temperature before serving.

Makes about 40 macarons.

MORE TO TRY:

To make **Mimmy Macarons**, attach two yellow heart-shaped sprinkles above the opposite ear.

Hello Kitty Jam-Filled Macarons: Short on time? Skip the frosting and fill macarons with strawberry jam. Warm jam in the microwave for a few seconds to achieve a smooth, spreadable consistency.

Hello Kitty Chocolate-Filled Macarons: Fill macarons with chocolate ganache or Nutella.

HELLO KITTY MERINGUE COOKIES

Mini meringue cookies shaped like Hello Kitty are perfectly bite-sized.
These melt-in-your-mouth confections are light, airy, and crisp (not to mention fat free).

3 egg whites
³/₄ cup sugar
¹/₄ tsp cream of tartar
¹/₂ tsp vanilla extract
Red heart-shaped sprinkles

Preheat oven to 225°F; line a baking sheet with parchment paper or a silicone baking mat. In the bowl of a mixer, combine egg whites, sugar, and cream of tartar. Place the mixer bowl over a pot of simmering water and whisk constantly until mixture reaches 150°F, or until sugar has dissolved. Attach the bowl to the mixer fitted with the whisk attachment and whisk until stiff peaks form. Add vanilla and continue whisking until mixture is glossy and the mixer bowl feels cool.

Fit a piping bag with a large round decorating tip and fill with the meringue. Pipe 1-inch-wide ovals about ¹/₂ inch apart on the baking sheet. Switch to a leaf tip and pipe two ears on top of each oval. Place two heart-shaped sprinkles to form a bow over one ear.

Bake for 40 minutes, then turn off the heat and let the meringues stay in the oven for one hour or until completely cooled. Store in an airtight container.

Makes about 100 meringue cookies.

TIPS: A candy thermometer helps determine when to take your egg whites off the heat. Other handy tools include a disposable piping bag, decorating tip couplers, a large round decorating tip, and a toothpick or leaf decorating tip (such as a Wilton #352 tip). ★ Don't throw away the unused egg yolks—save them for making ice cream!

HELLO KITTY
ICE CREAM SANDWICHES

These sweet treats are perfect for a hot summer day. The chocolate cookie is soft and just barely sweet, and complements the ice cream perfectly.

CHOCOLATE WAFER COOKIES

1 cup packed brown sugar
1 ³/₄ sticks butter
1 egg, room temperature
2 ¹/₂ cups all-purpose flour
¹/₂ cup dark or black cocoa powder
Pinch salt

COOKIES 'N' CREAM ICE CREAM

³/₄ cup sugar
4 egg yolks, room temperature
1 cup whole milk
2 cups heavy cream
Pinch salt
8 chocolate wafer cookies, roughly chopped

TO MAKE COOKIES: Combine brown sugar and butter in the bowl of a standing mixer. Beat with a paddle attachment until creamy. Add egg and mix on medium speed until combined. Sift flour, cocoa powder, and salt into mixture and mix until flour is incorporated and dough starts to come together in a large mass. Turn out dough onto a floured surface and flatten into a disk. Wrap in plastic wrap and chill in the refrigerator for at least 20 minutes.

Preheat oven to 350°F; line a baking sheet with parchment paper. Working on a floured surface, use a rolling pin to roll out dough to a ¹/₈-inch thickness. Use cookie cutters to cut out shapes and a stamper to press eyes, nose, whiskers, and bow into the cookie. Then use a large spatula to transfer the shapes to the baking sheet. Bake for 10 to 12 minutes. Let cool. Store in an airtight container at room temperature until ready to use.

TIPS: This recipe makes homemade ice cream, but you could use any store-bought flavor if you don't have an ice cream maker. ★ Use a Hello Kitty cookie cutter to cut out shapes for both the cookies and the ice cream. You could also use a Hello Kitty stamper to define features in the cookie if desired.

TO MAKE ICE CREAM: In a large bowl, whisk sugar and egg yolks until mixture is pale and creamy. In a medium saucepan, combine milk, heavy cream, and salt, warming over medium heat. Do not allow to boil.

While whisking the egg and sugar mixture, slowly ladle in the hot milk and cream mixture, a cup at a time. Then pour the entire mixture into the saucepan and cook over medium-high heat, stirring constantly with a heatproof rubber spatula. (Tip: Do not let the mixture come to a boil, which will curdle the eggs.) Keep stirring until the mixture thickens and coats the back of a spoon. Strain mixture into a large glass bowl and let it come to room temperature. Cover with plastic wrap and let custard chill in the refrigerator overnight.

Line two 8-inch round pans with plastic wrap. Churn custard in an ice cream maker for 25 to 30 minutes, until it resembles soft-serve. Fold in the chopped chocolate wafer cookies. Pour the ice cream evenly into the prepared pans, smoothing the top with an offset spatula. Cover with plastic wrap and freeze overnight.

TO ASSEMBLE: Lay cookies on a baking sheet or plate. Working quickly, use the cookie cutter to stamp out shapes from the ice cream, then use a spatula to transfer the ice cream cutouts onto the cookies. Top each one with a second cookie and immediately place in the freezer to set for at least one hour.

Makes about 16 to 20 ice cream sandwiches, depending on the cookie cutter.

MORE TO TRY:

To make **Chocolate Sandwich Cookies,** fill cookies with your favorite frosting or chocolate ganache instead of ice cream.

USE A TEMPLATE TO DUST CONFECTIONERS' SUGAR OVER BROWNIES FOR A QUICK AND EASY WAY TO ADD A HELLO KITTY IMAGE.

HELLO KITTY BROWNIES

These chocolate brownies are moist and chewy, and they have a classic crackly top.
They're quick and easy to whip up, and the best part is they can be made in just one bowl.

$^1/_3$ **cup cocoa powder**

$^1/_2$ **cup hot coffee**

2 ounces bittersweet chocolate chips

$^1/_4$ **cup ($^1/_2$ stick) unsalted butter, melted**

$^1/_2$ **cup plus 2 tbsp vegetable oil**

3 eggs

2 tsp vanilla extract

2 $^1/_2$ cups sugar

1 $^3/_4$ cups all-purpose flour

$^1/_2$ **tsp salt**

Confectioners' sugar, for dusting

Preheat oven to 350°F. Line a 9-by-13-inch baking pan with foil or parchment paper.

Whisk together cocoa powder and hot coffee in large bowl. Add chocolate chips and whisk until melted. Whisk in melted butter and oil. Add eggs and vanilla and continue to whisk until smooth. Whisk in the sugar. Add flour and salt and whisk until combined.

Pour batter into prepared baking pan and bake for 30 to 35 minutes, until a toothpick inserted into the center comes out clean. Let cool. Cut into 2-inch squares. Place the template over one square and dust with confectioners' sugar. Repeat for the remaining squares.

Makes 24 brownies.

MORE TO TRY:

For a fun alternative, make **Hello Kitty, My Melody, Hello Kitty's Bow, Flower,** or **Heart-Shaped Brownies** using the corresponding cutters to cut out shapes. Or make Round Bite-Sized Brownies by baking the batter in mini cupcake tins for 15 to 20 minutes.

TIP: Make a paper template to dust a Hello Kitty image with confectioners' sugar (how-to, page 87; templates, pages 88-89).

CAKES AND CUPCAKES

RED APPLE CUPCAKES ...32

MINI CHOCOLATE SWEETHEART CUPCAKES ...35

HELLO KITTY PERFECT PINK CAKE WITH CHOCOLATE
LAYERS AND STRAWBERRY FROSTING ...37

More to Try: Chococat Cake and Keroppi Cake

BADTZ-MARU COOKIES 'N' CREAM
ICE CREAM CAKE ...40

More to Try: My Melody and Hello Kitty Ice Cream Cakes

PRETTY BOW BIRTHDAY CAKE WITH STRAWBERRIES
AND WHIPPED CREAM FROSTING ...45

HELLO KITTY PINK OMBRÉ CAKE COVERED
WITH MINI HELLO KITTY FACES ...49

More to Try: Hello Kitty Pink Ombré Cupcakes

HELLO KITTY-SHAPED CAKE ...52

KEROPPI MINT CHOCOLATE CAKE ...55

More to Try: Hello Kitty and Chococat Mint Chocolate cakes

RED APPLE CUPCAKES

A bit of Hello Kitty trivia: She is as tall as five apples and weighs
the same as three apples! Decorated to look like the apples
they are made from, these cupcakes are the perfect fruity treat.

APPLE CUPCAKES

2 cups all-purpose flour

2 tsp cinnamon

2 tsp baking soda

1 tsp salt

$^1/_2$ cup vegetable oil

2 cups sugar

2 eggs

2 tsp vanilla

4 cups apples, diced in
 $^1/_4$-inch cubes

DECORATING

1 recipe Cream Cheese Frosting
 (page 35)

Gel-based food coloring (red)

2 dozen pretzel sticks

2 dozen light green taffy candies
 (such as Starburst or Air Heads),
 or green fondant

TO MAKE CUPCAKES: Preheat oven to 350°F.
Line a cupcake tin with paper liners.

In a medium bowl, sift together flour, cinnamon, baking soda,
and salt. In the bowl of a mixer, mix oil and sugar on medium
speed until well combined. Add eggs and vanilla and whisk
until incorporated. Add flour mixture in three batches,
whisking after each until just combined. Fold in the apples.

Fill the wells of the cupcake tin halfway with batter. Bake
for 20 to 25 minutes, until a toothpick inserted into the
center comes out clean. Let cool in the cupcake tin for 10
minutes, then transfer to a wire rack to cool completely.

TO ASSEMBLE: Add a few drops of food coloring
to the frosting. Frost the cupcakes. Press a pretzel stick
into the center of each cupcake. Roll the taffy candies or
fondant with a rolling pin until thin. Use a knife to cut out
leaves. Press a line into each leaf with the back of a knife
and pinch one end. Place a leaf on each cupcake.

To store, refrigerate for up to 2 to 3 days, bringing to
room temperature before serving.

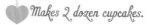 *Makes 2 dozen cupcakes.*

TIPS: Frost the cupcakes with a butter knife or offset spatula. Or use a piping bag with a large round tip to
pipe a big dollop on top of the cupcake. ★ You can use leaf-shaped cookie cutters for easier decorating.

MINI CHOCOLATE
SWEETHEART CUPCAKES

These bite-size cupcakes are moist, chocolaty, and topped with
tangy cream cheese frosting. Customize the colors to match any party theme!

CHOCOLATE CUPCAKES

$^1/_2$ recipe chocolate cake batter
(page 37)

CREAM CHEESE FROSTING

1 8-ounce package (1 cup) cream
cheese, room temperature
$^1/_4$ cup ($^1/_2$ stick) unsalted butter
3 cups confectioners' sugar, sifted
Pinch salt
1 tsp vanilla extract
Gel-based food coloring
(pink and red)

TO MAKE CUPCAKES: Preheat oven to 350°F.
Line a mini cupcake tin with paper liners. Fill each well
three-quarters with the batter. Bake for 15 to 20 minutes,
until a toothpick inserted into the center comes out clean.

TO MAKE CREAM CHEESE FROSTING:
Using a stand mixer fitted with the paddle attachment,
whip cream cheese and butter until creamy. Add sugar, salt,
and vanilla and beat until fluffy. Use immediately or cover
the bowl with plastic wrap and refrigerate, mixing briefly
(using the paddle attachment) before using.

TO DECORATE: Tint half of the frosting pink and
the other half red. Fit two disposable piping bags with
couplers and fill each with one color of frosting. Using
a medium round tip, pipe a teardrop shape on one side
of a cupcake. Repeat on the other side, connecting the
tapered ends to form a V. (Or pipe a heart outline and fill
with piped stars.) Use just one color per cupcake.

To store, refrigerate for up to 2 to 3 days, bringing to
room temperature before serving.

 Makes about 48 mini cupcakes.

TIPS: Have a medium round piping tip (such as Wilton #12) at the ready to pipe a plump heart onto each tiny
treat. ★ You will also need disposable piping bags and decorating tip couplers.

HELLO KITTY PERFECT PINK CAKE WITH CHOCOLATE LAYERS AND STRAWBERRY FROSTING

What could go better together than strawberries and chocolate? In this cake, moist cake layers are filled with fruity strawberry cream cheese frosting. I like to decorate with basket-weave sides, a rope border, and Hello Kitty on top. (If you're not big on piping decorations, ice the sides of the cake with an offset spatula; it'll look more like the cake on page 41.)

CHOCOLATE CAKE

1³/₄ cups all-purpose flour

2 cups sugar

³/₄ cups cocoa powder

2 tsp baking soda

1 tsp baking powder

1 tsp salt

1 cup whole milk

¹/₂ cup vegetable oil

2 eggs, room temperature

1 tsp vanilla extract

¹/₂ cup hot coffee

¹/₂ cup hot water

TO MAKE CAKE: Preheat the oven to 350°F. Butter and flour two 8-inch round cake pans, or coat with baking spray. Line with parchment paper (see page 85 for a quick how-to).

Sift flour, sugar, cocoa, baking soda, baking powder, and salt into a mixing bowl. Whisk until combined. In another bowl, lightly whisk milk, oil, eggs, and vanilla. Add the wet ingredients to the dry in three batches, whisking after each. Add hot coffee and water and stir until combined, scraping the bottom of the bowl with a rubber spatula.

Divide batter equally between the cake pans and bake for 35 to 40 minutes, until a toothpick inserted into the center of each cake comes out clean. Let cakes cool in the pans for at least 30 minutes, then invert them onto a cooling rack and cool completely.

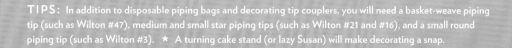

TIPS: In addition to disposable piping bags and decorating tip couplers, you will need a basket-weave piping tip (such as Wilton #47), medium and small star piping tips (such as Wilton #21 and #16), and a small round piping tip (such as Wilton #3). ★ A turning cake stand (or lazy Susan) will make decorating a snap.

STRAWBERRY FROSTING

1^1/$_2$ cups (3 sticks) unsalted butter, room temperature

6 cups confectioners' sugar

Pinch salt

3 tbsp water

1^1/$_2$ 8-ounce packages (1^1/$_2$ cups) cream cheese, room temperature

3 tbsp strawberry jam

Gel-based food coloring (red, yellow, and black)

Strawberry extract

TO MAKE FROSTING: Using an electric mixer fitted with the paddle attachment, whip butter until creamy. Add confectioners' sugar, salt, and water and beat until combined. Add cream cheese and whip until fluffy.

Set aside 1 cup of frosting (this will be used to pipe the Hello Kitty face). To the rest, add strawberry jam and a few drops of red food coloring and mix until combined. If you love strawberries, add a few drops of strawberry extract (Tip: If at any point the frosting seems too loose, place the entire mixer bowl of frosting in the refrigerator and let chill for 30 minutes or more. Do a quick rewhip before using.)

TO ASSEMBLE: Place 1 tablespoon of the reserved white frosting into a bowl and tint it with yellow food coloring. Divide the remaining white frosting among three bowls: leave ^{1}/$_2$ cup white, tint ^{1}/$_4$ cup with red food coloring, and tint 3 tablespoons with black food coloring. Fit piping bags with couplers and fill each with a color of frosting.

Place one cake layer on a cake board or cake stand. With just the coupler attached to the piping bag, pipe a ring of strawberry frosting around the perimeter of the top. Then place a big dollop in the middle of the ring, and use an offset spatula to smooth it out.

Place the other cake layer on top of the frosting layer. Cover the top and sides of the cake with strawberry frosting, smoothing it with an offset spatula. It is important for the top to have a thick, smooth frosting layer, but the sides can have only a thin layer (this is known as the crumb coat). Place cake in the refrigerator and let set for at least 30 minutes and up to overnight.

Fit a piping bag with a basket-weave tip and fill with strawberry frosting. Pipe a basket-weave design on the sides of the cake (see page 85 for how-to). Switch to a medium star tip and pipe a rope border on the top perimeter of the cake (see page 82 for how-to).

Draw Hello Kitty onto the top of the cake using a toothpick and a paper template (see page 88 for templates), or use a large cookie cutter to gently stamp the shape onto the cake. Use black frosting and a small round tip to pipe the outline of the face, bow, eyes, and whiskers. Fill in the eyes with black frosting. Use yellow frosting and a small round tip to pipe the nose.

Using white frosting and a small star tip, pipe stars inside the entire outline of the face (see page 82 for how-to). Use red frosting and a small star tip to fill in the bow. Then switch to a small round tip and fill in the nose with red frosting.

Refrigerate cake for up to 2 days. Bring to room temperature before serving.

Makes one 8-inch cake, serves 12 to 16.

MORE TO TRY:

To make a **Chococat Cake**, place 1 tablespoon of the reserved white frosting into a bowl and tint it with brown food coloring. Divide the remaining white frosting among four bowls: leave $1/4$ cup white, tint $1/2$ cup with black food coloring, and tint 3 tablespoons with yellow food coloring. Use black frosting and a small round tip to pipe the outline of the face, white frosting to outline and fill in the eyes, yellow frosting to outline and fill in the ears, and brown frosting to outline and fill in the nose. Then use a star tip with the black frosting to fill in the face with piped stars.

To make a **Keroppi Cake**, place 1 tablespoon of the reserved white frosting into a bowl and tint it with pink food coloring. Divide the remaining white frosting among four bowls: leave $1/4$ cup white, tint $1/2$ cup with green food coloring, and tint 3 tablespoons with black food coloring. Use black frosting and a small round tip to pipe the outline of the face, eyes, and mouth. Use white frosting and a star tip to fill in the eyes. Use pink frosting and a small round tip to outline and fill in the cheeks. Use a star tip with green frosting to fill in the face with piped stars.

BADTZ-MARU COOKIES 'N' CREAM ICE CREAM CAKE

If you've never had a homemade ice cream cake, you're in for quite a treat!
Moist chocolate cake, homemade cookies 'n' cream ice cream, and fresh chocolate whipped cream set this version apart from anything you'll find in the supermarket. Give yourself plenty of time to make this cake—the components need to be frozen overnight before assembly.

CHOCOLATE CAKE

¹/₂ **recipe chocolate cake batter (page 37)**

ICE CREAM

1 recipe cookies 'n' cream ice cream (page 24)

FROSTING

1 8-ounce package (1 cup) cream cheese, room temperature

¹/₂ cup sugar

2 tsp vanilla extract

Pinch salt

2 cups heavy cream, cold

5 tbsp cocoa powder, sifted

Black and yellow gel-based food coloring

TO MAKE CAKE LAYER: Bake as directed in an 8-inch round cake pan. Let cool completely. Wrap in plastic wrap and freeze overnight.

TO MAKE ICE CREAM LAYER: Line an 8-inch round pan with plastic wrap. Prepare ice cream as directed on page 26, but instead of dividing between two pans, pour the entire mixture into the cake pan. Smooth the top with an offset spatula. Cover with plastic wrap and freeze overnight.

TO MAKE FROSTING: In the bowl of a stand mixer fitted with the whisk attachment, whisk cream cheese, sugar, vanilla, and salt on medium-high speed until creamy. Reduce speed to low and slowly add heavy cream, mixing until incorporated, then increase speed to medium-high and mix until stiff peaks form. Place 1 cup of the frosting in the refrigerator. Add cocoa powder

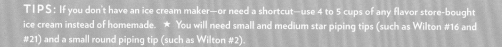

TIPS: If you don't have an ice cream maker—or need a shortcut—use 4 to 5 cups of any flavor store-bought ice cream instead of homemade. ★ You will need small and medium star piping tips (such as Wilton #16 and #21) and a small round piping tip (such as Wilton #2).

to the remaining frosting and whip on medium speed until incorporated, scraping down the sides of the bowl as necessary. Refrigerate until ready to use.

TO ASSEMBLE CAKE: Unwrap the frozen cake layer and place on a cake board. Unwrap the frozen ice cream layer and place on top of the cake layer. Return to the freezer to harden for at least 1 hour.

Working as quickly as possible so that the ice cream doesn't melt, cover top and sides of cake with chocolate frosting, smoothing it with an offset spatula.

Fit a piping bag with a medium star tip and fill with chocolate frosting. Pipe a shell border on the top and bottom perimeter of the cake (see page 84 for how-to). Return cake to the freezer.

Transfer $1/2$ cup of the 1 cup reserved white frosting to a small bowl and tint it with black food coloring (for the face). Transfer another $1/4$ cup of the reserved frosting to a bowl and tint it yellow (for the beak). Leave the remaining $1/4$ cup of reserved frosting white (for the eyes).

Fit three piping bags with couplers and fill each with one color of frosting.

Using a toothpick and a paper template (if desired), draw Badtz-Maru onto the top of the cake (see page 88 for templates). Use black frosting and a small round tip to pipe the outline of the face, the black parts of the eyes, and the line of the beak. Use white frosting and a small round tip to outline and fill in the whites of the eyes. Use yellow frosting and a small round tip to outline and fill in the beak.

Switch to a small star tip and black frosting and fill in the face with stars (see page 82 for how-to).

Freeze cake uncovered for up to 3 days. Let stand at room temperature for 30 minutes before serving.

Makes one 8-inch ice cream cake.

MORE TO TRY

To make **My Melody Ice Cream Cake,** prepare and frost the ice cream cake as instructed. Draw My Melody onto the top using a toothpick and a paper template.

TIP: If the ice cream starts to melt, refreeze cake for 30 minutes, or until hardened.

Tint 3 tablespoons of the reserved frosting with black food coloring, 1 tablespoon orange, and $1/2$ cup pink; leave $1/4$ cup white. Use black frosting and a small round tip to pipe the outlines of the bow, oval face, and hood and ears. Outline and fill in the eyes and add the mouth. Use orange frosting and a small round tip to outline and fill in the nose. Use white frosting and a small star tip to fill in the bow and face with stars. Use pink frosting and a small star tip to fill in the hood and ears with stars.

To make **Hello Kitty Ice Cream Cake**, see Perfect Pink Hello Kitty Cake (page 37) and follow the instructions for piping Hello Kitty's face.

PRETTY BOW BIRTHDAY CAKE
WITH STRAWBERRIES AND
WHIPPED CREAM FROSTING

This combination of fresh, delicate flavors—vanilla cake, whipped cream,
and fresh strawberries—will please kids and adults alike. For an equally delicious cake,
replace the strawberries with blueberries or raspberries. The pretty bow on top
and festive rainbow sprinkles make this cake perfect for a birthday celebration.

VANILLA CAKE

- $1/2$ cup (1 stick) unsalted butter, room temperature
- $1^3/4$ cups sugar
- 4 egg whites, room temperature
- 1 tsp vanilla extract
- 1 tsp almond extract
- 2 cups plus 2 tbsp cake flour
- $3^1/2$ tsp baking powder
- $1/2$ tsp plus $1/8$ tsp baking soda
- 1 tsp salt
- $1/2$ cup whole milk
- 1 cup (8 ounces) sour cream

Preheat oven to 325°F. Butter and flour two 8-inch round cake pans, or coat with baking spray. Line with parchment paper (see page 81 for how-to).

TO MAKE CAKE: In the bowl of a standing mixer, whisk butter and sugar at medium speed until creamy. Add egg whites, vanilla, and almond extract. and mix until incorporated. In a medium bowl, sift flour, baking powder, baking soda, and salt. Alternate adding the flour mixture and the milk in 3 batches, mixing after each until just combined. Fold in sour cream until incorporated.

Pour batter into the cake pans and bake for 35 to 40 minutes, until a toothpick inserted into the center of the cake comes out clean. Cool in the pans for at least 30 minutes, then invert onto a cooling rack to cool completely.

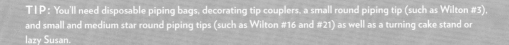

TIP: You'll need disposable piping bags, decorating tip couplers, a small round piping tip (such as Wilton #3), and small and medium star round piping tips (such as Wilton #16 and #21) as well as a turning cake stand or lazy Susan.

FROSTING

2 8-ounce packages (2 cups)
cream cheese, room temperature

1 cup sugar

4 tsp vanilla extract

Pinch salt

4 cups heavy cream, cold

Gel-based food coloring
(black, red, pink)

ASSEMBLING AND DECORATING

1 pint fresh strawberries,
sliced thinly

2 to 3 tbsp rainbow sprinkles

TO MAKE FROSTING: In the bowl of a standing mixer, whisk cream cheese, sugar, vanilla, and salt until creamy. With the mixer on low speed, slowly add heavy cream until incorporated, then increase speed to medium-high until stiff peaks form.

TO ASSEMBLE: Use a serrated knife to slice each cake in half horizontally (see page 87 for how-to) to create 4 layers. Place the first layer on a cake board or cake stand. With just the coupler attached to the piping bag, pipe a ring of whipped cream around the perimeter of the cake. Then place a big dollop of in the middle of the ring and use an offset spatula to smooth it evenly. Lay the sliced strawberries in an even layer on top of the whipped cream, leaving a $1/2$-inch border. Cover with another dollop of whipped cream and use an offset spatula to smooth it evenly. Place the second cake layer on top of the strawberries and whipped cream layer and repeat until all the cake layers are used. (Hint: You will not add whipped cream and strawberries to the last layer because the top of the cake will be frosted.)

Tint about $1/4$ cup of the whipped cream with black food coloring, and tint another $1/4$ cup red. Tint the remaining frosting pink. Fit 3 piping bags with 3 couplers and fill each with one color of frosting. Cover the top and sides of the cake with pink whipped cream, smoothing it with an offset spatula. Chill in the refrigerator for 30 minutes, then repeat with another coat of whipped cream. Use the large star tip to pipe a shell border on the top and bottom of the cake (see page 84 for a how-to).

Using a toothpick, draw a bow onto the top of the cake, either freehand or using a template (page 87). Use a small round tip and black frosting to pipe the bow outline. With red frosting and a small star tip, pipe stars to cover the entire bow area except the inside loops (see page 82 for how-to). Use red frosting and a small round tip to fill in the loops. Add rainbow sprinkles to the top and bottom shell border. Refrigerate cake for up to 2 days. Bring to room temperature before serving.

Makes one 8-inch cake, serves 12 to 16.

HELLO KITTY PINK OMBRÉ CAKE

I made this cake for my own birthday one year—and it was everything I could ask for. Four layers of varying shades of pink cake are filled with a chocolate cream cheese filling and covered with fluffy Swiss meringue buttercream frosting. A multitude of Hello Kitty faces decorate the sides, and the cake is topped off with a perfect red bow.

PINK CAKE LAYERS

1 recipe vanilla cake batter (page 45)
A few drops of gel-based food coloring

CHOCOLATE CREAM CHEESE FILLING

1 8-ounce package (1 cup) cream cheese, room temperature
1/4 cup (1/2 stick) butter, at room temperature
1 tsp vanilla extract
Pinch salt
3 cups confectioners' sugar, sifted
4 tbsp cocoa powder

TO MAKE CAKE: Preheat the oven to 325°F. Butter and flour four 6-inch round cake pans or coat with baking spray. Line with parchment paper.

Prepare cake batter and divide it among 4 bowls. Leave one portion white; tint the other three varying shades of pink, each successively darker to create the ombré effect. Fill each cake pan with one shade of batter. Bake for 25 to 30 minutes, until a toothpick inserted into the center comes out clean. Cool cakes in pans for at least 30 minutes, then invert them onto a cooling rack, remove parchment, and cool completely.

TO MAKE FILLING: Using a mixer fitted with the paddle attachment, whip cream cheese and butter on medium-high speed until creamy. Add vanilla, salt, confectioners' sugar, and cocoa powder and whip until fluffy.

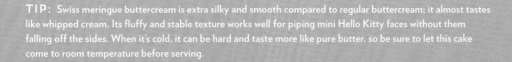

TIP: Swiss meringue buttercream is extra silky and smooth compared to regular buttercream; it almost tastes like whipped cream. Its fluffy and stable texture works well for piping mini Hello Kitty faces without them falling off the sides. When it's cold, it can be hard and taste more like pure butter, so be sure to let this cake come to room temperature before serving.

SWISS MERINGUE BUTTERCREAM FROSTING

5 egg whites

1 cup plus 2 tbsp granulated sugar

1 1/2 cups (3 sticks) unsalted butter, room temperature and cut into chunks

1 tsp vanilla extract

Pinch salt

Gel-based food coloring (black, red, yellow)

TO MAKE FROSTING: Combine egg whites and sugar in a mixer bowl. Place mixer bowl over a pot of simmering water, attach a candy thermometer to the side, and whisk the mixture constantly but gently until the temperature reaches 150°F or until the outside of the bowl is warm and the sugar has dissolved. Remove from heat. Fit mixer with the whisk attachment and whisk on high speed until the mixture holds stiff peaks. Continue whisking until the mixture becomes glossy and the outside of the bowl feels cool. Switch to the paddle attachment. With the mixer on medium-low speed, add butter one chunk at a time. Then add vanilla and salt and continue beating on medium speed until the mixture is smooth.

TO ASSEMBLE: Using a serrated knife, slice off the top so that each layer is about 1 inch tall. Place the white cake layer on a cake board or cake stand. Transfer filling to a piping bag fitted with just a coupler and pipe a ring around the top perimeter of the cake. Then place a big dollop in the middle of the ring and use an offset spatula to smooth it evenly. Next place the lightest pink cake layer and repeat with the filling. Repeat with the medium and darkest pink cake layers, piping filling between each.

Divide the frosting into 4 bowls: Tint about 1/4 cup with black food coloring for the eyes and whiskers. Tint 1/3 cup red for the bows. Tint 1/4 cup yellow for the noses. Leave the rest white. Fit 4 piping bags with 4 couplers and fill each with one color of frosting.

Cover the cake top and sides with white frosting, smoothing it with an offset spatula. Chill for 30 minutes, then repeat with another coat of white frosting.

With just the coupler attached to the piping bag (or you could use a large round tip), pipe a vertical row of four 1-inch ovals. Repeat all the way around the cake. Switch to a leaf tip (such as Wilton #352) and pipe two triangles for ears on top of each oval.

With black frosting and a small round tip (such as Wilton #2), add eyes and whiskers. With red frosting and a small round tip, add bows. With yellow frosting and a small round tip, add noses.

Using a toothpick, draw the bow onto the top of the cake, either freehand or using a paper template (page 89). Use black frosting and a small round tip to pipe the bow outlines. Then use red frosting and a small round tip to pipe the inner circular part of the bow. Switch to a small

star tip (such as Wilton #16) to fill in the rest of the bow (see page 82 for how to pipe stars). Refrigerate for up to 3 days. Bring to room temperature before serving.

Makes one 4-layer 6-inch cake, serves 8 to 10.

VARIATION

To make **Hello Kitty Pink Ombré Cupcakes**, line cupcake tin with paper liners. Prepare batter with varying shades as directed and pour one shade of batter into each prepared cupcake tin until $^3/_4$ full. Bake at 350°F for 18 to 20 minutes, until a toothpick inserted into the center comes out clean. Let cool. Frost with varying shades of pink frosting, and pipe a Hello Kitty face (page 86) on each.

HELLO KITTY SHAPED CAKE

This cake looks spectacular but is actually easy to decorate. Two layers of chocolate cake are sandwiched with freshly whipped cream and covered with a tangy cream cheese frosting to create a 3-D Hello Kitty face! You can customize the bow and nose to any color you like.

CHOCOLATE CAKE

2 ²/₃ cups all-purpose flour

3 cups sugar

1 cup good-quality cocoa powder

3 tsp baking soda

1 ¹/₂ tsp baking powder

1 ¹/₂ tsp salt

1 ¹/₂ cups whole milk

³/₄ cup vegetable oil

3 eggs, room temperature

1 ¹/₂ tsp vanilla extract

³/₄ cup hot coffee

³/₄ cup hot water

FILLING, FROSTING, AND DECORATING

1 cup heavy cream, chilled

¹/₂ cup confectioners' sugar, sifted

1 tsp vanilla extract

(continued)

TO MAKE CAKE: Preheat oven to 350°F. Butter and flour pan, or coat with baking spray.

Sift flour, sugar, cocoa powder, baking soda, baking powder, and salt into a mixing bowl. Whisk until combined. In another bowl, lightly whisk milk, oil, eggs, and vanilla. Add wet ingredients to dry ingredients in three batches, whisking after each addition. Add hot coffee and water and stir until combined, scraping the bottom of the bowl with a rubber spatula.

Pour half the batter into the cake pan and bake for 40 to 45 minutes, until a toothpick inserted into the center of the cake comes out clean. Cool in pan for at least 30 minutes, then invert onto a cooling rack to cool completely. Wash and recoat the cake pan and bake the other half of the batter.

TO MAKE FILLING: Place cream, sugar, and vanilla to the mixing bowl of a stand mixer. Using the whisk attachment, whip until the cream can hold a stiff peak.

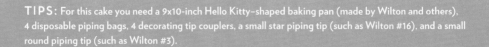

TIPS: For this cake you need a 9x10-inch Hello Kitty–shaped baking pan (made by Wilton and others), 4 disposable piping bags, 4 decorating tip couplers, a small star piping tip (such as Wilton #16), and a small round piping tip (such as Wilton #3).

HINT: THIS RECIPE IS FOR A TWO-LAYER CAKE, BUT IT LOOKS EQUALLY AS IMPRESSIVE WITH JUST ONE LAYER. JUST MAKE HALF THE BATTER AND FROSTING AND OMIT THE FILLING.

1 ¹/₂ **recipes cream cheese frosting (page 35)**

Gel-based food coloring (black, red, yellow)

TO ASSEMBLE: Divide the frosting into 4 bowls: Tint ¹/₄ cup of the frosting black for the eyes, whiskers, and bow outline. Tint ¹/₂ cup red for the bow. Tint ¹/₄ cup yellow for the nose. The rest will remain white. Fit piping bags with couplers and fill each with one color of frosting.

Place one cake layer on a cake board or stand. Use a serrated knife to slice off the elevated portion, leaving a flat surface. With just the coupler attached to the piping bag of white frosting, pipe an outline around the cake perimeter. Then place a dollop of whipped cream inside the outline and use an offset spatula to smooth it evenly (you may not need all of the whipped cream).

Place the other cake layer on top of the whipped cream layer. The top of the cake should have the elevations of Hello Kitty's face. Cover the top and sides with a light crumb coat of white frosting, smoothing it with an offset spatula. (Tip: It does not need to be perfectly smooth—it will be covered with piped stars later.)

Following the indentations on the top of the cake, use black frosting and a small round tip to pipe the outline of Hello Kitty's eyes, bow, and whiskers. Fill in the eyes with black frosting. Use yellow frosting and a small round tip to pipe the outline of the nose and fill it in. Then use red frosting and a small round tip to pipe the inner circular part of the bow. Switch to a small star tip to fill in the rest of the bow (see page 82 for how to pipe stars).

Using white frosting and a small star tip, pipe stars to cover the rest of the cake, including the sides. Refrigerate the cake for 2 to 3 days. Bring to room temperature before serving.

Makes one 9-by-10-inch cake, serves 20 to 30.

KEROPPI MINT
CHOCOLATE CAKE

This Keroppi-shaped confection is made with moist chocolate cake
and creamy, refreshing minty filling and frosting.

1 recipe chocolate cake (page 37),
   baked in two 8-inch cake pans

1 recipe whipped cream frosting
   (page 46)

1¹/₂ tsp peppermint extract

Gel-based food coloring (green,
   black, pink)

Prepare the frosting and stir in 1¹/₂ teaspoons peppermint extract. Tint ¹/₃ cup of the frosting with black food coloring, ¹/₃ cup with pink, and set aside ¹/₂ cup frosting to remain white. Tint the remaining frosting green. Fit 4 piping bags with 4 couplers and fill each with a frosting color.

Place the template on each cake and cut out the shape of Keroppi. Use a serrated knife to slice each cake in half horizontally to make 4 layers (see how-to on page 87). Place one layer on a cake board or stand. With just the coupler attached to the piping bag of green frosting, pipe a ring around the cake perimeter. Then place a big dollop in the middle of the ring and use an offset spatula to smooth it evenly. Place another layer on top and repeat with the frosting until all the layers are used. Cover the cake top and sides with a thin coat green frosting, smoothing it with an offset spatula. Chill in the refrigerator for 30 minutes.

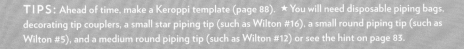

TIPS: Ahead of time, make a Keroppi template (page 88). ★ You will need disposable piping bags, decorating tip couplers, a small star piping tip (such as Wilton #16), a small round piping tip (such as Wilton #5), and a medium round piping tip (such as Wilton #12) or see the hint on page 83.

HINT: TO DECORATE THE EASY WAY, SPREAD GREEN FROSTING TO COVER THE CAKE TOP AND SIDES. USE PINK SPRINKLES FOR THE CHEEKS, WHITE SPRINKLES FOR THE EYES, AND CHOCOLATE SPRINKLES FOR THE PUPILS AND MOUTH.

Using a toothpick and a template, draw Keroppi's eyes, mouth, and cheeks onto the cake. With the black frosting and a medium round piping tip, pipe the outline for the eyes, fill in the inner eyeballs, and pipe the mouth. Use pink frosting and a small round tip to pipe and fill in the cheeks. Use white frosting and a small star tip to fill in the eyes (see page 82 for how to pipe stars). Use green frosting and a small star tip to cover the cake top and sides with piped stars.

Refrigerate the cake for up to 2 days. Bring to room temperature before serving.

Makes one 7-inch cake, serves 10 to 12.

VARIATIONS

To make a **Hello Kitty Mint Chocolate Cake**, use a Hello Kitty template on each cake and cut out the shapes. Use black frosting and a small round tip to pipe the outline of the bow, eyes, and whiskers; yellow frosting and a small round tip to pipe and fill the nose; and red frosting and a small star tip to fill in the bow. Use white frosting to cover the cake top and sides with piped stars.

To make a **Chococat Mint Chocolate Cake**, use the Chococat template on each cake and cut out the shapes. Use white frosting to outline and fill in the eyes; yellow frosting to outline and fill the ears; and brown frosting to outline and fill in the nose. Then switch to a star tip and black frosting to cover the cake top and sides with piped stars.

PIES, PARTY TREATS, AND MORE

HELLO KITTY AND FRIENDS
CAKE POPS

Moist and decadent bites of chocolate cake are covered with a candy coating shell and decorated to look like Hello Kitty and her friends. These treats-on-sticks make great party favors and add an extra dose of cuteness to any dessert table.

1 8-inch **Chocolate Cake** layer (page 37), baked and chilled

1 cup **Cream Cheese Frosting** (page 35)

¹/₂ cup **Royal Icing** (page 13)

About 1¹/₂ cups (12 oz) white chocolate chips

About 36 lollipop sticks

Gel-based food coloring (yellow, black)

About 2 tbsp red heart-shaped sprinkles

Line a baking sheet with parchment paper. Make the cake, frosting, and icing.

TO MAKE CAKE BALLS: Place cake in a food processor and pulse into crumbs. Place in a large bowl with frosting and stir with a rubber spatula until all the crumbs are moist and you can no longer see the frosting. Scoop out 1-tablespoon portions of the cake mixture and roll into balls with your hands. Place on the baking sheet and refrigerate for at least 30 minutes, until firm.

TO DECORATE: Set aside 72 white chocolate chips (about ¹/₄ cup). Melt the rest in a double boiler or heatproof bowl set over a saucepan of simmering water, stirring constantly. (Tip: If the melted chocolate seems too thick, stir in a teaspoon or so of vegetable shortening to thin it.) Dip one end of each lollipop stick into the melted white chocolate and then insert it into a cake ball. Repeat until all the cake balls are on sticks.

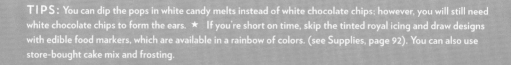

TIPS: You can dip the pops in white candy melts instead of white chocolate chips; however, you will still need white chocolate chips to form the ears. ★ If you're short on time, skip the tinted royal icing and draw designs with edible food markers, which are available in a rainbow of colors. (see Supplies, page 92). You can also use store-bought cake mix and frosting.

AS HELLO KITTY ALWAYS SAYS, YOU CAN NEVER HAVE TOO MANY FRIENDS! MAKE CAKE POPS OF HER FRIENDS (PAGES 62-63) AND EXPERIMENT TO CREATE YOUR OWN CHARACTERS.

HINT: USE UPSIDE-DOWN WHITE CHOCOLATE CHIPS TO MAKE EYES FOR KEROPPI AND OTHER CHARACTERS.

Using a toothpick, dab a bit of melted white chocolate onto the bottom of a white chocolate chip and place it on a cake ball, pressing gently to adhere. Continue until all the pops have two ears.

Dip each cake pop into the melted chocolate. Gently tap the lollipop stick on the side of the double boiler while twirling it between your fingers to remove excess melted white chocolate. Using a toothpick, dab a bit of melted white chocolate on the bottom of two heart-shaped sprinkles and place them above one ear to make the bow. Let pops dry upright and uncovered at room temperature for about 1 hour.

Divide icing between 2 bowls: Add a few drops of yellow food coloring to 2 tablespoons of icing in one bowl and a few drops of black food coloring to the remaining icing in the other. Fit piping bags with couplers and small round tips and fill each with one icing color.

Use black icing to pipe on eyes and whiskers and yellow royal icing to pipe on a nose. Let dry for at least 1 hour. Refrigerate cake pops in an airtight container until ready to serve.

Makes about 36 cake pops.

MORE TO TRY

My Melody Cake Pops: You will need about 1 ¼ cups (10 ounces) pink candy melts. Use 72 pill-shaped candies (such as Hot Tamales or Mike and Ike) to make the ears by inserting 2 of them into the top of each cake pop (dip the end of each candy in pink coating before inserting). Dip cake pops in pink coating and let dry. Then dip just the front of the cake pops in white royal icing (or pipe it on) for the face. Use black royal icing to draw the eyes and mouth, and use yellow royal icing for the nose; alternatively, you can use black and yellow edible food markers to create the face.

Chococat Cake Pops: Set aside 72 white chocolate chips (about ¼ cup) to make the eyes. Substitute about 1 ¼ cups (10 ounces) black candy melts for the remaining white chocolate chips. You will need 72 chocolate chips for the ears; dab a bit of melted candy coating on the bottom of each and press gently into cake ball to adhere. Dip cake pops in coating and then quickly, before coating dries, attach 2 white chocolate chips as eyeballs, the flat side facing out. Attach 2 chocolate sprinkles on each side for whiskers. Let dry. Use black royal icing to draw the eyes and mouth, yellow royal icing for the ears, and brown royal icing for the nose.

Keroppi Cake Pops: Set aside 72 white chocolate chips (about $1/4$ cup) to make the eyes. Substitute about $1 1/4$ cups (10 ounces) green candy melts for the remaining white chocolate chips. Dip cake pops in coating and then quickly, before coating dries, attach 2 white chocolate chips as eyeballs, the flat side facing out. Let dry. Use black royal icing to draw the eyes and mouth and pink royal icing for the cheeks; alternatively, you can use black and pink edible food markers to create the face. You could also use round pink confetti sprinkles for cheeks.

Badtz-Maru Cake Pops: Set aside 72 white chocolate chips (about $1/4$ cup) to make the eyes. Use a knife to cut $1/4$ off the side of each chip, so that you are left with large half circles. Substitute about $1 1/4$ cups (10 ounces) black candy melts for the remaining white chocolate chips. Use 144 rainbow chips or mini chocolate chips (about $1/3$ cup) to make 4 spikes on each cake pop (dip each in coating to attach them). You will also need 36 orange rainbow chips for the beak (or you could pipe the beak with orange royal icing). Dip cake pops in black coating and then quickly, before coating dries, attach 2 eyes and the beak (if using rainbow chips). Let dry. Use black royal icing to draw the darks of the eyes, and orange royal icing to pipe the beak (if not using rainbow chips).

HELLO KITTY'S
FAVORITE APPLE PIE

Did you know that apple pie is Hello Kitty's favorite food?
This one has a buttery, flaky crust surrounding sweet cinnamon-scented apples.

CRUST

2 ¹/₂ cups all-purpose flour

2 tsp sugar

1 tsp salt

1 cup (2 sticks) cold butter,
  cut into small cubes

¹/₂ cup ice water

APPLE FILLING

4 cups apples, peeled and
  cut into ¹/₄-inch slices

1 cup sugar

3 tbsp all-purpose flour

1 tsp ground cinnamon

¹/₄ tsp ground cloves

¹/₄ tsp salt

ASSEMBLY

1 egg

2 tbsp water

1 tbsp sanding sugar

TO MAKE CRUST: In a large mixing bowl, mix flour, sugar, and salt and whisk until just combined. Add cold butter and use a pastry cutter to cut it into the flour mixture until the mixture is the size of small peas. Add 2 tablespoons of ice water and stir gently until absorbed. Continue to add ice water 2 tablespoons at a time until dough stays together when pinched (you may not need to use all of the water). Turn out dough onto a floured surface and use your hands to bring it together. Wrap tightly in plastic wrap and refrigerate for at least 30 minutes.

TO MAKE FILLING: Add apples, sugar, flour, cinnamon, cloves, and salt to a medium mixing bowl. Using a spoon or a spatula, stir until combined and apples are evenly coated. Set aside.

TO ASSEMBLE: Divide chilled dough in half and place half on a floured surface. Using a rolling pin, roll

TIP: Substitute store-bought pie crust and canned pie filling for a quick and easy treat.

out to a $1/8$-inch thickness and press into a 9-inch pie pan. Pour filling into the pie pan. Roll out the other half of the dough and carefully place on top of the filling. Trim excess dough and reserve. (Store in the refrigerator until ready to use.) Use your fingers or the tines of a fork to press and seal the dough edges. Cut 4 to 6 slits in the top crust to allow steam to escape during baking.

In a small bowl, use a fork to lightly whisk the egg and water together. Brush the top crust with egg wash and sprinkle with sanding sugar.

Preheat oven to at 425°F. Roll out the excess dough and use a Hello Kitty cutter to cut out as many shapes as you can. To create the face, press the stamp that comes with the cutter into the dough. (If your cutter did not come with a stamp, gently press a round piping tip into the dough to make the eyes and nose and draw a bow outline with a toothpick.) Use a spatula to place the cutouts onto the top of the pie; brush with more egg wash. Sprinkle sanding sugar over the entire pie.

Bake for 15 minutes, then lower the temperature to 350°F. Cover crust edges with aluminum foil and bake for another 50 to 60 minutes, until golden brown. Let cool before serving.

Makes one 9-inch pie.

VARIATION: To make individual **Hand-Held Apple Pies**, you'll need only half the recipe for the filling, with the apples diced into $1/4$-inch cubes. Roll out half the dough and use a large Hello Kitty cookie cutter to cut out shapes. Use a spatula to transfer the shapes to a baking sheet lined with parchment paper. Spoon enough filling to cover each cutout, leaving a 1-inch border. Roll out the other half of the dough and cut out an equal number of shapes. Create Hello Kitty's face as described above. Place the cutouts over the apple-topped pieces, lining up the shapes. Crimp the edges by pressing the tines of a fork into the dough. Brush tops with egg wash and sprinkle with sanding sugar. Bake at 350°F for 25 to 30 minutes, until golden brown.

HELLO KITTY AND PRETTY BOW STRAWBERRY-RHUBARB TARTLETS

Hello Kitty and her pretty bow go together like strawberry and rhubarb! These individual tartlets have a flaky crust and are filled with sweet and tangy strawberry rhubarb filling.

½ recipe pie crust (page 65)

1 ½ cups fresh strawberries, cut into small pieces

1 ½ cups fresh rhubarb, cut into small pieces

¼ cup sugar

2 tbsp all-purpose flour

Pinch salt

1 egg, for wash

1 tbsp water

Sanding sugar, for dusting

TO PREP DOUGH: Divide dough into 6 even pieces. One at a time, roll out each piece into a 1/8-inch-thick circle. Press into tartlet pan, rolling the rolling pin over the top of the pan to cut off excess dough. After all pans have been prepared, gather excess dough into a ball, wrap with plastic wrap, and refrigerate.

TO FILL AND BAKE: Preheat oven to 350°F. Place strawberries and rhubarb in a medium bowl. Add sugar, flour, and salt and toss until fruits are evenly coated. Spoon the filling evenly into tartlet pans.

Roll out the chilled excess dough and use cookie cutters to cut out shapes. Use the stamper (if using) to press facial details into the cutouts. Use a toothpick to create holes for the eyes and nose. Place one cutout on top of each tartlet. In a small bowl, use a fork to lightly whisk together the egg and 1 tablespoon of water. Brush over the cutouts and exposed crust; dust with sanding sugar. Place tartlets on a baking sheet and bake for 45 to 50 minutes, or until golden brown. Cool before serving.

TIPS: You'll need six 4-inch tartlet pans (or one 9-inch tart pan) and Hello Kitty and Pretty Bow cookie cutters or templates (page 87). ★ You can use Hello Kitty and My Melody stampers to define the facial features. (A toothpick works well, too.)

Makes 6 individual tartlets.

MORE TO TRY:

To make this into one large **Hello Kitty Strawberry-Rhubarb Tart** instead of individual tartlets, press dough into a 9-inch tart pan, spoon in filling, and arrange cutouts on top. Bake at 350°F for 1 hour. You can also substitute the strawberries with cherries for a delicious **Cherry-Rhubarb Tart**.

HELLO KITTY
PUMPKIN TART

What better way to add cheer to the holidays than with a Hello Kitty
pumpkin tart? A crispy crust and smooth, sweetly spiced filling are
topped with crispy crust cutouts in fun shapes.

PUMPKIN TART

$^1/_2$ **recipe pie crust (page 65)**
1 egg, for wash
Sanding sugar
1 cup canned pumpkin puree
$^1/_4$ **cup plus 2 tbsp sugar**
$^1/_2$ **tsp ground cinnamon**
$^1/_8$ **tsp ground nutmeg**
$^1/_8$ **tsp ground cloves**
$^3/_4$ **cup evaporated milk**

TO PREP CRUST: On a floured surface, roll out pie dough to just under $^1/_8$ inch thick. Carefully press it into the tart pan and roll the rolling pin across the top of the pan to cut off excess dough. Gather excess dough into a ball, cover in plastic wrap, and refrigerate it and the prepared tart crust for at least 15 minutes.

TO FILL AND BAKE: Preheat oven to 375°F; line a baking sheet with parchment paper. Roll out the chilled excess dough to just under $^1/_8$ inch thick and use cookie cutters to cut out 2 or 3 shapes; you can use a stamper or toothpick to press facial details into the cutouts. Transfer cutouts to the baking sheet. In a small bowl, use a fork to lightly whisk the egg and water together. Brush over cutouts. Sprinkle with sanding sugar and bake for 7 to 10 minutes, until golden brown. Cool.

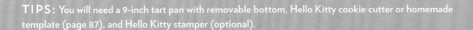

TIPS: You will need a 9-inch tart pan with removable bottom, Hello Kitty cookie cutter or homemade template (page 87), and Hello Kitty stamper (optional).

Increase oven temperature to 425°F. Whisk to combine pumpkin puree and egg. Whisk in sugar, cinnamon, nutmeg, and cloves. Add evaporated milk and whisk to combine. Pour pumpkin mixture into the tart crust and bake for 15 minutes. Lower oven temperature to 350°F and bake for another 35 minutes. Arrange cutouts on top of the tart and press them gently. Cool for at least 2 hours. Serve when cooled, or refrigerate if serving the next day.

Makes one 9-inch tart.

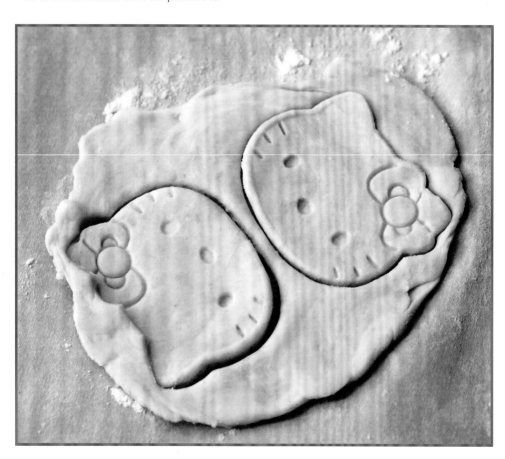

USE COOKIE CUTTERS OR DIY TEMPLATES
FOR FUN, DECORATIVE SHAPES (PAGE 88).

RAINBOW FINGER JELLO

This easy-to-eat treat is inspired by Hello Kitty's multicolored world.
You simply stack colorful fruity and creamy white cloud layers. Give yourself lots of
time because you will need to wait for each layer to set before adding the next.

COLOR LAYERS

1 (3-ounce) box red Jello
1 (3-ounce) box green Jello
1 (3-ounce) box purple Jello
1 (3-ounce) box blue Jello
2 packets unflavored gelatin
4 cups boiling water

WHITE LAYERS

2 packets unflavored gelatin
$1/2$ cup cold water
1 (14-ounce) can sweetened
    condensed milk
$1 1/2$ cups boiling water

TO PREP COLOR LAYERS: Place one box of Jello in each of 4 medium bowls. Stir $1/2$ packet of unflavored gelatin into each bowl and then add 1 cup boiling water to each, stirring until Jello dissolves.

TO PREP WHITE LAYERS: In a small bowl, sprinkle 2 packets unflavored gelatin over cold water and stir to dissolve. In a large bowl, stir to combine and dissolve sweetened condensed milk, the gelatin mixture, and boiling water.

TO ASSEMBLE: Lightly coat a silicone mold or baking pan with cooking spray or a bit of vegetable oil applied with a pastry brush. If you're using a mold, add a few spoonfuls of the first color to each mold, refrigerate for 30 minutes, and repeat, alternating colors and white layers. If you're using one pan, pour the entire colored layer each time, alternating with 1 cup of the white layer. When all layers have set, unmold (separate the sides from the mold and then pop one end out, using your fingers to pull it out) or use cookie cutters to cut shapes out of the pan. Serve immediately or refrigerate up to 3 days.

Makes 24 to 36 pieces.

TIPS: You can pour Jello into specially shaped silicone ice trays to make the Hello Kitty shapes, or you can make it in a 9-by-13-inch pan and use cookie cutters to cut out shapes. ★ If your unused gelatin mixtures start to set while waiting for their turn, microwave for 30 seconds and stir to return them to a pourable state.

HELLO KITTY MINI CHEESECAKES

These adorable little cheesecakes are big on flavor, from the delicious
chocolaty graham cracker crust to the fruity jam topping. Perfect for picnics
or parties, these are irresistible and yet so easy to make!

CRUST

1 cup ground chocolate graham crackers (from about 6 whole sheets)

2 tbsp melted butter

FILLING

3 8-ounce packages (3 cups) cream cheese, room temperature

1 $1/2$ cups sugar

1 tsp vanilla extract

Pinch salt

3 large eggs, room temperature

DECORATING

$3/4$ cup strawberry jam

3 tbsp confectioners' sugar, for dusting

Preheat oven to 350°F. Line the wells of a cupcake tin with paper liners and set aside a rimmed baking sheet or roasting pan with sides at least 2 inches high.

TO MAKE CRUST: In a medium bowl, combine ground graham crackers with melted butter. Add about 2 teaspoons of the mixture to each well of the lined cupcake tin, pressing it evenly with the back of a spoon. Bake for 5 minutes, or until set. Cool.

TO MAKE FILLING: Lower oven to 325°F. Bring about 6 to 8 cups water to a boil, and then cover and keep warm to use later for baking cheesecakes in a hot water bath. In the bowl of a mixer fitted with the whisk attachment, beat cream cheese on medium-high speed 2 to 3 minutes, until fluffy. Add sugar, vanilla, and salt and continue to mix well, about 2 to 3 minutes, until creamy, pausing often to scrape down the sides of the bowl. Add eggs one at a time, mixing after each addition until combined. Pour about $1/4$ cup of filling mixture over each crust in the cupcake tin. Tap the entire tin on the counter or smooth the tops with an offset spatula.

Place cupcake tin on the rimmed baking sheet or roasting pan and add just enough hot water to the baking sheet to submerge the cupcake tin about halfway. Bake for 20 to 25 minutes, until cheesecakes are set and just barely jiggly in the center. Remove cupcake tin from the water bath and cool cheesecakes in the tin on a cooling rack. (Tip: Remove the baking sheet from the oven once the water has cooled. It's easier that way.)

Warm jam in a saucepan over medium heat, stirring occasionally until it starts to melt and become runny. Spoon about 1 teaspoon of jam over each cheesecake. Refrigerate cupcake tin and let cheesecakes set for at least 3 hours.

Just before serving, place the Hello Kitty template (page 88) over each cheesecake and dust with confectioners' sugar using a shaker or fine-mesh sieve.

Makes 24 mini cheesecakes.

PIES, PARTY TREATS, AND MORE

BASIC BAKERY
HOW-TOS

Here are some of the basic techniques
that will make the process easy and the results spectacular.
Experiment with them and don't forget, practice makes perfect!

1. Use scissors to cut off a piece of parchment paper roughly the width of your cake pan. Fold up one corner to form a triangle so that the bottom of the paper is aligned with the side of the paper.

2. Cut off excess paper. Fold the triangle in half and in half once more. Place the center point of the triangle in the center of your pan. Use your finger to crease the paper against the corners of the pan where the sides meet the bottom.

3. Cut the paper along the crease. Unfold and place in the bottom of the pan to make sure it fits before using.

BASIC PIPING

1. Using a small round tip and stiff royal icing, squeeze the piping bag gently and outline the cookie. This will act as a border for the thinned icing.

2. Fill a decorating squeeze bottle with thin royal icing and fill in the outlined shape. You can use a toothpick to spread the icing to the border of the stiff icing.

3. After the icing has dried (a few hours or overnight), use a small round tip and stiff royal icing to outline the cookie once more.

PIPING STARS

1. Fit piping bag with a star tip (such as Wilton #16). Hold the piping bag perpendicular to the cake surface. Squeeze gently to force out the frosting.

2. Stop squeezing, then gently lift the piping bag straight up and away.

3. Continue piping stars next to one another to fill the entire area.

1. Fit piping bag with a star tip (such as Wilton #21). Squeeze bag gently to push frosting out while making a sideways S shape.

2. Pipe another sideways S shape, starting inside the bottom curve of the first S shape.

3. Continue piping sideways S shapes joined to the previous S, going all the way around the cake and stopping at the first S.

1. Fit piping bag with a star tip (such as Wilton #21). Squeeze bag hard to let the frosting fan out of the tip.

2. Lift the tip slightly up and away, then down, while gently releasing pressure to form a point. Stop squeezing and lift the tip away.

3. Start the next shell at the tail of the previous shell. Continue piping shells all the way around, stopping at the first shell.

1. Fit piping bag with a basket-weave tip (such as Wilton #47). Pipe a vertical line from top to bottom of the surface you want to cover. Pipe a short horizontal line across the vertical line to make a T. Continue piping horizontal lines down the length of the vertical line, with spacing the same width as the tip.

2. Pipe another vertical line, covering where the horizontal lines end.

3. Pipe another set of horizontal lines to fit in the gaps from the first set of horizontal lines, starting at the first vertical line and going over the second vertical line. Repeat alternating one vertical line with sets of horizontal lines, each set fitting between the previous set.

1. Fit piping bag with a decorating coupler (or you could use a large round tip). Pipe an oval about 1 inch wide. Switch to a leaf tip (such as Wilton #352) and pipe two triangles for ears on top of each oval.

2. With black frosting and a small round tip (such as Wilton #2), add eyes and whiskers.

3. With red frosting and small round tip, add bow (or you could use red heart-shaped confetti sprinkles). With yellow frosting and small round tip, add nose.

MAKING A TEMPLATE

1. Copy or print your image onto heavy paper or cardstock.

2. If using the template to cut out a shape, use scissors to cut out the shape from the paper. Place the template on top of the dessert (cake, dough, etc.), and use a knife to cut around the template.

3. If using the template for dusting or defining features, use a paper or craft knife to cut out the open lines or shapes. Place the template on top of the dessert and use a shaker or fine-mesh sieve so that the dusting powder passes through the cut lines or shapes. Gently remove the template.

SLICING A CAKE LAYER IN HALF HORIZONTALLY

1. Center the cake layer in the middle of a cake stand. Hold a serrated knife to the side of the cake, about halfway up, and lightly score the surface while slowly turning the stand.

2. When the cake has turned full circle, repeat, this time applying a little more pressure with the knife to slice deeper into the cake while turning the stand.

3. Continue applying more pressure while turning the cake until the knife has reached the center of the cake and the layer has been divided horizontally.

TEMPLATES

HELLO KITTY

KEROPPI

MY MELODY

CHOCOCAT

BADTZ-MARU

HELLO KITTY'S BOW

BAKING MATH

AMERICAN	IMPERIAL	METRIC
$^1/_4$ tsp	-	1.25 ml
$^1/_2$ tsp	-	2.5 ml
1 tsp	-	5 ml
$^1/_2$ tbsp ($1^1/_2$ tsp)	-	7.5 ml
1 tbsp (3 tsp)	-	15 ml
$^1/_4$ cup (4 tbsp)	2 fl oz	60 ml
$^1/_3$ cup (5 tbsp)	$2^1/_2$ fl oz	75 ml
$^1/_2$ cup (8 tbsp)	4 fl oz	125 ml
$^2/_3$ cup (10 tbsp)	5 fl oz	150 ml
$^1/_2$ cup (12 tbsp)	6 fl oz	175 ml
1 cup (16 tbsp)	8 fl oz	250 ml
$1^1/_4$ cups	10 fl oz	300 ml
$1^1/_2$ cups	12 fl oz	350 ml
1 pint (2 cups)	16 fl oz	500 ml
$2^1/_2$ cups	20 fl oz (1 pint)	625 ml
5 cups	40 fl oz (1 qt)	1.25 L

OVEN TEMPERATURES	°F	°C	GAS MARK
Very cool	250–275	130–140	$^1/_2$ –2
Cool	300	148	2
Warm	325	163	3
Medium	350	177	4
Medium hot	375–400	190–204	5–6
Hot	425	218	7
Very hot	450–475	232–245	8–9

SUPPLIES

CAKE, CUPCAKE, AND COOKIE DECORATING

You will find cake boards, piping bags, decorating tips, candy coatings, and other decorating supplies at specialty baking shops, grocery stores, and culinary boutiques. Here are a few tried-and-true online vendors.

Wilton: www.wilton.com

Confectionery House: www.confectioneryhouse.com

CRAFT STORES

Craft retailers often carry some bakeware and lots of great decorating supplies, edible gift wrapping materials, and other handy tools.

Michaels: www.michaels.com

Jo-Ann Fabric and Craft Stores: www.joann.com

A.C. Moore: www.acmoore.com

Hobby Lobby: www.hobbylobby.com

Etsy: www.etsy.com

COOKIE CUTTERS AND DOUGH STAMPERS

Available from countless retailers, unique cookie cutters and stampers are always fun to hunt for.

Wilton: www.wilton.com

Ebay: www.ebay.com

FOOD COLOR AND EDIBLE-INK PENS

Gel-based food color and edible-ink pens (a.k.a. markers) can be found at specialty baking stores and the following online sources:

Wilton: www.wilton.com

Americolor: www.americolorcorp.com

PANS FOR CAKES, COOKIES, PIES, TARTS, AND TARTLETS

Wilton: www.wilton.com

Williams-Sonoma: www.williams-sonoma.com

SPRINKLES

Confectionery House: www.confectioneryhouse.com

Sur La Table: www.surlatable.com

INDEX

References to photographs are in **bold**.

94

ACKNOWLEDGMENTS

This book is dedicated to my family and friends, and to Hello Kitty lovers. Thank you!
Without you, this book would not have been possible.

Thank you to my husband, Grant, for being so supportive and encouraging. Words cannot express how much I love you, and how grateful I am to have you on this adventure right beside me. To my babies, Matthew, Melodie, and Micah (my Three Musketeers!), for being such awesome kids, and for being my inspiration behind baking new and fun things. To my Mom, for teaching me how to bake, and for all your love and guidance throughout all of these years. To my brother Michael, and to all of my cousins, for taste-testing at family get-togethers and always encouraging me. To my cousin Angie, for inspiring me and believing in me—you predicted that I would write a book before I thought it was even remotely possible! To my wonderful girlfriends, Sue, Regina, Diana, Helen, Cecila, and Naomi, thank you for putting up with my baking ramblings and experiments; I'm so lucky to have you girls in my life! To our neighbors and co-workers, for always eating my "mistakes and mess-ups." To Margaret McGuire, for finding me and getting me involved in this project. To my talented book designer Amanda Richmond, for designing such a beautiful, adorable, and fun book. To Steve Legato, for a beautiful cover and amazing shots, and such a fun photoshoot. To the Quirk staff, for making all of this possible. To all the readers of my blog, I Heart Baking!, thank you for reading my blog and for following me on my baking journey. And finally to Hello Kitty and her friends, thank you for always making me smile!

Thank you all so much for making this book possible!

FOR BONUS RECIPES
AND MORE HOW-TOS,
Visit
QUIRKBOOKS.COM/
HELLOKITTYBAKINGBOO